Generations Rock

Gaining the Generational Advantage

Karen McCullough

Generations Rock

Gaining the Generational Advantage

Willard St. Publishers
Houston, TX

By Karen McCullough

Published by Willard St. Publishers
Printed in the United States of America
thesevenwomenproject.com

Author:	Karen McCullough
Contributors:	Meredith McCullough, Angie Noel
Book Cover Design:	Lisa Thomson
Book Design:	Mike Svat

13-digit ISBN: 978-0-9837541-2-1
9-digit ISBN: 0-9837541-2-8
Library of Congress Control Number: 2010921762

1. Business – Psychology 2. Sales – Success
First Edition: August 2017

For Campbell, Connally, Emory, Jack and Ben.

Members of Generation Z

With joy I look forward to watching you grow, evolve and contribute to the world.

Contents

"Once I was seven years old my momma told me
Go make yourself some friends or you'll be lonely
Once I was seven years old

Once I was twenty years old, my story got told
Before the morning sun, when life was lonely
Once I was twenty years old

I only see my goals, I don't believe in failure
Cause I know the smallest voices, they can make it major
I got my boys with me at least those in favor
And if we don't meet before I leave, I hope I'll see you later

I'm still learning about life
My woman brought children for me
So I can sing them all my songs
And I can tell them stories
Most of my boys are with me
Some are still out seeking glory
And some I had to leave behind
My brother I'm still sorry

Soon I'll be sixty years old, my daddy got sixty-one
Remember life and then your life becomes a better one
I made a man so happy when I wrote a letter once
I hope my children come and visit, once or twice a month

Soon I'll be sixty years old, will I think the world is cold
Or will I have a lot of children who can warm me
Soon I'll be sixty years old
Soon I'll be sixty years old, will I think the world is cold
Or will I have a lot of children who can warm me
Soon I'll be sixty years old"

Lyrics from "7 years"
by Lukas Forchhammer
Sung by Lukas Graham – 2015

"It's time to begin, isn't it?
I get a little bit bigger but then I'll admit
I'm just the same as I was
Now don't you understand
I'm never changing who I am
It's time to begin, isn't it?"

Lyrics from "It's Time"
Mckee, Reynolds, Sermon
Sung by Imagine Dragons – 2010

A Word from Karen...

Hi there. Welcome to *Generations Rock*. I am really happy you decided to pick up this book on the generations. I hope you like it!

Honestly, I have been thinking about writing a book on the generations for the last 10 years. I have given countless talks and breakout sessions on the topic, read and researched and read some more, and authored my fair share of blog posts. But I have never gotten around to actually doing any more than just thinking about writing a book. In fact, I may have never pulled all my knowledge and experience together for this book at all if it hadn't been for a little bit of outside motivation.

Around November 2016, I received a call from an organization looking for a speaker to present on the generations. The event planners explained that they wanted something different from the usual and somewhat academic presentation of the topic. They were looking for more pizzazz—a more fun, more inspiring, more interactive keynote so engaging that it might even appeal to the younger folks in the audience (guests of their moms). Their hope was that the younger generation would enjoy the day so much that they would up and join the organization. No pressure.

They asked me if I could create this kind of fun and motivational keynote on the generations…and if so, asked what I would call it.

Well, I have always loved pop culture and music in particular. In my programs, I look for ways to add games and find a prominent place for music. Recently I visited the Rock and Roll Hall of Fame in Cleveland, Ohio and I saw how music transcends boundaries, celebrates differences, overcomes biases, and ultimately brings people together.

"Generations Rock!" I blurted out. They loved the title. Then they asked if I had a book.

Without missing a beat, I said, "Yes!"

And I started writing.

Acknowledgements

The truth is *Generations Rock* could not have gone from concept to reality without the input, help, and overall support of so many wonderful people.

First – my audiences! Women and men from all generations have listened to my programs and shared with me their thoughts, stories, and experiences. To be fair, many have disagreed with what I've had to say… which has allowed me to see some of my unconscious biases and has opened my mind to new ways of seeing and doing things.

I want to thank my Generation X son, Ben, who keeps me humble, reminding me that it's not always the "Karen Show."

I want to thank my daughter Meredith (another Xer) who, in addition to being my writing muse and design architect, continues to share new ways to look at the world.

Both my sisters, Patty and Terry, shared their great insights as Traditionalists, growing up in the era of college beanies, big bands, jazz, and beatniks.

Angie Noel, thank you for your friendship and your writing contribution. Your involvement in this project has expanded my understanding of the future of work!

This book may have never happened if it wasn't for Sue Falcon, Remarkable Speakers Bureau, asking me if I had a book to go along with my keynote. Talk about a motivator!

Thank you Hanna Healey, for our in-depth phone calls. You are my "Millennial insider," sharing your work experiences, opening my eyes to the Millennial work ethic as well as current fashion tips.

Mike Svat, you pulled through for me! For your ongoing support and immediate save, formatting this book on top of your busy schedule (and wedding) I am supremely grateful.

Eliot Perez, you are my personal motivator. Not only do raise my daily spirits that keep me writing, you also have introduced me to current music, that helped me find the right lyrics for the book.

I need editors—I'm a speaker…so, boy do I need editors!—and Joy Seeman, you have been working with me for years. I love—and appreciate—your comments and your perspective.

Leslie Randall, aka the "Comma Queen" (and my poker buddy), I appreciate your suggestions, corrections and your speedy turnaround!

Lisa Thomson, I love the cover you designed and your continued support and ideas, helping make this book ROCK!

And finally—a hardy thank you to my readers, my fellow speakers and my speaker mastermind group, Vicki, Jana, Rebecca, Barbara, who continue to share their wisdom, encouragement, and most importantly, friendship. Thank you all!

"Hey Mister D.J.
Put a record on
I want to dance with my baby
Hey Mister D.J.
Put a record on
I want to dance with my baby
And when the music starts
I never want to stop
It's gonna drive me crazy
Music
Music makes the people come together
Music makes the bourgeoisie and the rebel"

Lyrics from "Music" by Madonna
Sung by Madonna – 2000

Introduction

The Beginning

I started my speaking career in 2000. Coming from a fashion retail background, my early programs focused on success, professionalism, and "The Look of Leadership." At that time, what people wore to work was beginning to change as younger employees (emerging as Generation X) pushed to relax the dress code in the workplace. Human Resource departments across the country began to offer "casual dress" as a perk their companies could use to attract this talented, younger generation. In response to this trend, I created programs that helped organizations define the "right look" for their industry. It was a start, but I wasn't really thinking about these young people beyond what they were wearing (and the two I was raising—Meredith and Ben).

And I wasn't alone. As you may have guessed, I am what they call a Baby Boomer, and in true Boomer fashion, didn't really think much about the other generations early in my career. After all, did any other generations really matter?

That mindset began to shift for me around 2004. I remember, because for me, it was while I watching *American Idol* on television. For those of you who may not remember, *American Idol* (all 15 seasons!)

is a competitive singing competition series where hundreds of young hopefuls sing in front of three judges (originally Simon Cowell, Paula Abdul, and Randy Jackson), but only a fraction make it to Hollywood, and are selected to compete in the show.

Though the eligible age range for contestants has been adjusted over the years, participants were from about 15 to 28 years old.

Season to season, the TV viewing audiences have witnessed some pretty horrible performances during the nights of the first screenings. Over and over, judges turn down wannabe stars, and America watches as the dejected contestants walked out of the screening room...and into the arms of their parents waiting outside for them.

Time after time, even the most tone-deaf singer's parents say, "They missed out on the next superstar" or "I just can't believe you didn't make it!"

For contestants who make it past those early rounds, as they get closer and closer to the final goal, they are at the mercy of not just the judges, but also of the viewing public itself. Viewers are invited to call—or text—their vote for their preferred performer. After Season 10, votes could also be cast online.

And it was from watching this play out over the years that I began to recognize more clearly this new generation on the horizon. Generation Y—a generation whose parents were their biggest supporters, who were highly individualistic, enjoying attention and fame, and who were connected to each other through technology.

My signature line in the early days was, "Gen Y: the first generation whose self-esteem is greater than their talent."

I don't say that today, Millennials! Honest!

Things were changing and life was getting very interesting. Once I began to put the pieces together... Boomers, Gen Xers, Millennials...oh my! My new speech, *Generations in the Workplace*, was born!

"People try to put us d-down
(Talkin' 'bout my generation)
Just because we get around
(Talkin' 'bout my generation)
Things they do look awful c-c-cold
(Talkin' 'bout my generation)
I hope I die before I get old
(Talkin' 'bout my generation)

This is my generation
This is my generation, baby

Why don't you all f-fade away
(Talkin' 'bout my generation)
Don't try to dig what we all s-s-s-say
(Talkin' 'bout my generation)
I'm not trying to cause a big s-s-sensation
(Talkin' 'bout my generation)
I'm just talkin' 'bout my g-g-g-generation
(Talkin' 'bout my generation)

My generation
This is my generation, baby

Why don't you all f-fade away
(Talkin' 'bout my generation)
And don't try to d-dig what we all s-s-say
(Talkin' 'bout my generation)
I'm not..."

Lyrics from "My Generation"
by Peter Townshend
Sung by The Who – 1965

What Makes a Generation?

By definition, a generation is a group of people born around the same time, grouped into a 15-20-year lifespan. Generations are decided by demographics, common attitudes, habits, and behaviors. You might think of it as an automatic membership into a club of "like-minded" individuals.

Traditionalist:	***1930 – 1945***
Baby Boomer:	***1946 – 1964***
Gen X:	***1965 – 1980***
Millennial:	***1981 – 2001***

Fueling the interest in generations is the idea that an individual's age is one of the most common predictors of differences in attitudes and behaviors. Not the only predictor, of course, but one of the most common ones. When studying the different generations, age directly points to a person's place in the life cycle—young adult to retiree—and suggests that there are some characteristics that are shared among people born at a similar time.

Age gives us a place to start the study as researchers track a generation of people over the course of their lives. In addition to age, there are several other distinct factors that help define a generation, such as the national and world events that occurred in the group's collective formative years, prevalent parenting styles and trends, and use of technology, pop culture and shifting of attitudes, to name a few. When studied as a group, each generation shares a similar set of characteristics, preferences, work ethics, and values.

The biggest challenge is putting all people born between certain dates into one group, because we are all unique and each of us may experience different situations that help shape who we are and how we respond to the world around us. Sometimes a person from one generation has experiences more closely associated with those experiences of someone from a different generation. For example, a Boomer whose mom worked—a "latchkey kid"—may have similarities to a Generation Xer. These variables may put a person into a different generation's mindset and they may be a hybrid of two or even three generations.

AND now we have a new generation on the horizon. Gen Z, anyone?

Researchers have noticed that generation-shaping trends seem to come into play when individuals enter the workplace. That is, young adults begin to express similar values, beliefs, and expectations they may have developed and shared while they were younger.

Remember, as mentioned above, ultimately each person is different, and making broad generalizations about a person can lead you down the wrong path.

Asking questions while getting to know a person is the best indicator of a person's preferences. But looking at people through a generational lens offers useful predictability for those trying to reach, inform, or persuade a large cross-section of a population.

Understanding what drives generational differences strengthens our understanding of how public attitudes are being shaped and offers an indication of what the future holds for each of us!

"I got my first real six-string
Bought it at the five-and-dime
Played it 'til my fingers bled
Was the summer of sixty-nine
Oh, when I look back now
That summer seemed to last forever
And if I had the choice
Yeah, I'd always wanna be there
Those were the best days of my life

And now the times are changin'
Look at everything that's come and gone
Sometimes when I play that old six-string
I think about you, wonder what went wrong

Standin' on your mama's porch
You told me that it'd last forever
Oh, and when you held my hand
I knew that it was now or never
Those were the best days of my life

Oh, yeah
Back in the summer of sixty-nine, oh
It was the summer of sixty-nine, oh, yeah
Me and my baby in sixty-nine, oh
It was the summer,
the summer,
the summer of sixty-nine, yeah"

Lyrics from "Summer of Sixty Nine"
Bryan Adams
Sung by Adams – 1985

Dates Matter...Kind Of

Here is the breakdown of the generations and a timeline of national and world events that occurred during each one. By looking at this you can get a good picture of why each generation is uniquely different from the others. This list also includes key advances in technology (national only) that were made during this time.

National and world events that occurred during the Traditionalist time period

1928 – Stock market crash
1929 – President Herbert C. Hoover
1929 – 1939 The Great Depression
1930 – Beginning of the "Golden Age of Radio"
1933 – President Franklin D. Roosevelt
1933 – 1938 The New Deal
1935 – Social Security Act passes
1935 – First phone call made around the world
1939 – 1945 WWII
1941 – Attack on Pearl Harbor
1945 – President Harry S. Truman
1945 – Atomic bomb dropped on Japan
1945 – WWII ends

During the Boomer time period

1947 – Beginning of the rise of U.S. corporations
1950 – Korean War
1951 – Black and White TV in U.S. homes
1951 – First direct dial phone coast to U.S. coast
1953 – President Dwight D. Eisenhower
1954 – 1968 Civil Rights Movement
1955 – Polio vaccine/Jonas Salk
1956 – Elvis Presley appears on the Ed Sullivan TV Show
1958 – 1st American satellite Explorer 1 launched into space
1957 – Russia's Sputnik launched—dawn of the space era
1959 – NASA announces 7 military pilots 1st US Astronauts
1960 – Beginning of Counterculture/Sexual Revolution
1961 – President John F. Kennedy
1961 – 1st American troops arrive in Vietnam
1961 – Word Processor by IBM introduced
1962 – Astronaut John Glenn makes 1st U.S. orbit
1963 – Assassination of Kennedy
1963 – President Lyndon Baines Johnson (LBJ)
1963 – Touch-tone phones
1964 – Passage of Civil Rights Act
1964 – Color TV in many U.S. homes
1964 – 8-Track tapes
1964 – The Beatles appear on the *Ed Sullivan Show*

During the During Gen X time period

1965 – Assassination of Malcolm X
1968 – Assassination of Martin Luther King
1968 – Assassination of Robert Kennedy
1968 – Women's Liberation Movement
1969 – President Richard M. Nixon
1969 – Walk on the moon by John Glenn
1969 – Woodstock
1872 – Munich Olympics terrorist attacks

1973 – Watergate
1974 – Richard Nixon resigns
1974 – President Gerald R. Ford
1975 – Vietnam War comes to an end
1974 – Arab oil embargo
1977 – President James (Jimmy) E. Carter
1978 – Jonestown
1979 – Iran hostages and Energy Crisis
1980 – John Lennon assassinated

During the Millennial time period

1981 – President Ronald W. Reagan
1981 – AIDS identified
1981 – Space Shuttle Columbia is launched
1986 – Space Challenger disaster
1987 – Black Monday stock market crash
1989 – Pan Am flight 103 crashes
1989 – Exxon Valdez oil spill
1989 – Fall of the Berlin Wall
1989 – President George H. W. Bush
1990 – Desert Storm – Gulf War
1993 – President William (Bill) J. Clinton
1993 – Dot-com era begins
1995 – OJ trial
1995 – Oklahoma City bombing
1997 – Death of Diana, Princess of Wales
1998 – Google opens
1999 – Columbine shootings
1999 – Wi-Fi
1999 – The Blackberry
1999 – TiVo allows us to watch TV when we want
1999 – MySpace launches
2000 – PlayStation 2
2000 – Bluetooth introduced
2001 – President George W. Bush

2001 – Attack on the World Trade Center – 911
2001 – War in Afghanistan
2001 – Wikipedia
2001 – IPod
2001 – Xbox released
2001 – Facebook

"And now, the end is near
And so I face the final curtain
My friend, I'll say it clear
I'll state my case, of which I'm certain
I've lived a life that's full
I've traveled each and every highway
But more, much more than this
I did it my way
Regrets, I've had a few
But then again, too few to mention
I did what I had to do
And saw it through without exemption
I planned each charted course
Each careful step along the byway
And more, much more than this
I did it my way
Yes, there were times, I'm sure you knew
When I bit off more than I could chew
But through it all, when there was doubt
I ate it up and spit it out
I faced it all and I stood tall
And did it my way"

Lyrics from
"My Way" by Paul Anka
Sung and Popularized by
Frank Sinatra – 1968

Is There a Little Traditionalist in You?

- ☐ I believe that hard work and even some sacrifice makes us all better people.
- ☐ I am a saver and I save for today and for the future of my family.
- ☐ I enjoy doing things with my hands such as knitting, woodworking, baking, and so on.
- ☐ I am what you might call a "lurker" on social media. I like to read what others are doing and I especially enjoy following my grandkids.
- ☐ I turn the light off when leaving a room.
- ☐ Just like Jimmy Fallon, I too write "Thank You Notes" and would love to get one from you!
- ☐ I prefer a good home cooked meal to dining out in restaurants.
- ☐ I still have a landline and I enjoy a daily phone conversation or two.
- ☐ I have a variety of musical favorites that include the big bands, jazz, and Frank Sinatra.
- ☐ I am very patriotic and I love my country.
- ☐ Respect is something I believe we could all use a little more of when it comes to our leaders, police, teachers, and elders.

Who is the Traditionalist?

Born 1930 – 1945

Tough Times, Sacrifice, and Hard Work

The Traditional Generation—also known as the "Veterans," the "Silent Generation," and the "Greatest Generation"—is comprised of men and women born between 1930 and 1945. This group not only survived the Great Depression, but they also brought the nation out of World War II (WWII) and helped make the United States a world power. Patriotism, teamwork, sacrifice, "doing more with less," and task-orientation very much define this generation. Rules of order, respect for authority, and following directions are all important touch points for Traditionalists.

When it comes to technology, this generation has had to adapt. The only entertainment they grew up with were the voices coming out of a box—the radio. They were raised sitting around a radio with their family listening to spellbinding stories, like "The Shadow," "Dick Tracy," "Lux Radio Hour," and "Our Miss Brooks," which filled their evenings with suspense and entertainment.

When we think about the wonder of those times, it was their minds that created the pictures they heard from the voices on the radio. There was no TV or video games—maybe that is where the genius of Walt Disney was nourished. Although Disney was born before the Traditionalists in 1901, he was still part of an era when people relied on their own imaginations for entertainment.

Words of Wisdom: How many of these do you remember hearing?

Traditionalists were also raised listening to their parents spouting proverbs that centered on work, patience, and delayed gratification. These proverbs were a part of the Traditionalist's DNA, and they quoted them often to their own children.

Keep your personal to-do list short.

- A bird in the hand is worth two in the bush.
- A penny saved is a penny earned.
- Better safe than sorry.
- Don't count your chickens before they're hatched.
- Don't cry over spilt milk.
- Early to bed and early to rise makes a man healthy, wealthy, and wise.
- If at first you don't succeed, try, try again.
- Never put off 'til tomorrow what you can do today.
- Practice makes perfect.
- The early bird catches the worm.
- The grass is always greener on the other side of the fence.
- Waste not, want not.
- What goes around, comes around.
- You can lead a horse to water, but you cannot make him drink.

NASA, Medicine, and Equality

The Traditionalist generation spawned the first true innovators. They were responsible for developing NASA, which has led to today's space program. Back in the 1950s, NASA chose seven men (astronauts) who would fly on the Mercury spacecraft and called these men the "Mercury Seven." John Glenn, one of them, was the first American to orbit the earth in 1962.

Traditionalists also created vaccines for many diseases including polio, tuberculosis, tetanus, and whooping cough, laying the foundation for today's technological environment in healthcare.

This generation was the first to pursue equality through the Civil Rights Movement that began in the mid 50s with protests against racial segregation and discrimination. The movement began by attempting to tear down the inherent discrimination in public facilities that segregated blacks from whites.

As the movement expanded, the struggle for freedom and reform extended to economic, political, and cultural arenas. Dr. Martin Luther King Jr., a Baptist minister, lead the Civil Rights Movement from the mid 1950s until his assassination in 1968.

Good-bye to Traditions

Traditionalists may be the last generation to help pass on the individual family traditions. Growing up, my sisters and I loved our family traditions. Coming from an Italian family background, we knew that every Sunday we would have either homemade lasagna or tortellini or, maybe, rigatoni...and always meatballs. At Christmas, my mom made tins of homemade cookies, breads, and our favorite—almond biscotti. My mom loved special family dinners and set a fancy table with the family china, crystal, and silver.

Every Thanksgiving we counted on Mom to make the stuffing recipe exactly the same—and we would get really upset if she added anything extra like mushrooms or sausages. My dad would carve the turkey with the special knife reserved for Thanksgiving and Christmas. Regrettably, as time has marched on, many of our family traditions have gone by the wayside.

When Baby Boomers, the children of Traditionalists, began to develop their own lifestyles, families changed. Many from Generation X, the children of Boomers, share memories of holidays described as a "happy blur" with a "working mom" doing some frenzied cooking and cleaning, along with the dreaded car trips from one relative's house to the next. If the relatives all lived in the same city, Thanksgiving could possibly be two or three huge meals packed into one day.

When Generation X moved out of the house (be it for college, job, marriage) many of them continued these traditions by traveling home and spending a few days or a week at the parents' home from Christmas Day to New Year's Day. Movies such as National Lampoon's Christmas Vacation (1989), Home for the Holidays (1995), and Four Christmases (2008) capture well those hectic years.

When Generation X married, another "holiday issue" was set into play: deciding which family gets to host them, followed by the travel arrangements and subsequent tight sleeping quarters. Many Xers admit that they would break their parents' hearts if they didn't come home for Christmas. But, the question is often, how do they decide on which family to go to?

After the grandchildren arrive on the scene, numerous Xers and now Millennials often decide to forgo many of their past traditions and begin traditions of their own, but admit they still call Grandma to get all the delicious family recipes.

If your grandparents are still with you, take time to ask them to share ideas and traditions with your family and try to keep some of those important customs alive.

Key Attributes of Traditionalists

- Loyal
- Contributor
- Dedicated
- Their Word is their bond
- Patriotic
- Hard-working
- Strong work ethic
- Makes sacrifices
- Patient
- Responsible

Traditionalists are influenced by these factors

- The Depression
- WWII
- Korean War
- New Deal
- GI Bill
- Elvis and Rock and Roll
- The Civil Rights Movement

Movies that Define the Traditionalists

- *Casablanca*
- *Citizen Kane*
- *It's a Wonderful Life*
- *The Maltese Falcon*
- *Key Largo*
- *Double Indemnity*
- *Singing in the Rain*
- *The Wizard of Oz*
- *North by Northwest*
- *Rear Window*
- *Street Car Named Desire*
- *All About Eve*
- *Gone with the Wind*
- *Grapes of Wrath*
- *It Happened One Night*
- *On the Waterfront*
- *Vertigo*
- *Some Like It Hot*
- *The Philadelphia Story*
- *My Fair Lady*
- *All Quiet on the Western Front*
- *The Best Years of Our Lives*

Traditionalists Who Rock

- *Mick Jagger*
- *Brian Wilson*
- *Aretha Franklin*
- *Graham Nash*
- *Paul McCartney*
- *Paul Simon*
- *Bob Dylan*
- *Neil Diamond*

- *Smokey Robinson*
- *Carole King*
- *Debbie Harry*
- *Keith Richards*
- *Frankie Valli*
- *David Crosby*
- *Little Richard*
- *Eric Clapton*
- *Roger Daltrey*
- *Marvin Gaye*
- *Tina Turner*
- *Barbra Streisand*
- *Rod Stewart*

What the Traditionalist Wants Today

- *To change the image of aging*
- *Prefers these terms: "older" or "senior citizen"—"retired" is OUT and "experienced" is IN*
- *Respect*
- *Security*
- *To focus on their experience*
- *To leave a legacy*
- *Honoring their decisions*
- *Health and a sense of well-being*
- *To be remembered—give them a call or drop by*

"If I was the question, would you be my answer?
If I was the music, would you be the dancer?
If I was the student, would you be the teacher?
If I was the sinner, would you be the preacher?

Would you be my
N' dun d-dun dun

I still got a lot of shit to learn, I'll admit it
N' dun d-dun dun
I still got a lot of shit to learn, I'll admit it"

Lyrics from
"Lot to Learn" by Luke Christopher
Sung by Christopher — 2017

A Closer Look at a Traditionalist Who Rocks

Paul the Intern

In 2015, a movie, *The Intern*, was released, telling the story of a 70-year old retired gentleman named Ben (played by Robert DeNiro) who applied for an internship at an online fashion retailer...and got hired! The story unfolds showing the audience the "Traditionalist work ethic" of the elderly intern. Ben is driven, demanding, smart, dynamic, and a workaholic!

The Intern was not only a fun movie to watch, but also inspiring and it caught the eye of Sally Susman. Sally always wanted to bring an experienced Traditionalist or Boomer into the mix with the Millennial interns! Sally headed up the communications at Pfizer and the movie got Sally thinking about a retired executive she knew named Paul Critchlow. In his lifetime Paul served in Vietnam, was a reporter for the Philadelphia Inquirer, served as spokesperson for a Pennsylvania governor and spent the last 30 years of his life working in communications for Merrill Lynch.

Sally knew Paul from a past project and invited him to lunch under the pretense of "picking his brain" for advice. A bit nervous, she finally asked Paul the big question, "Would you consider being my summer intern?" After some discussion Paul agreed to be her intern for the standard intern pay scale of $18.25 an hour.

When the big first day on the job arrived, Paul decided to wear what he always wore to work, a suit, tie, white shirt, polished shoes, and briefcase. He was nervous and so were the three interns (dressed business casual) who were to share their workspace with Paul. The

Millennial interns were trying to check Paul out on LinkedIn, but had a hard time finding him on any of the social media sites because he didn't have a profile.

As the first day progressed they learned more about each other. Paul took a small group of interns to a sushi lunch, where he shared stories about his time in Vietnam and that he is still recovering from shrapnel wounds from a rocket-propelled grenade attack. "Wow, you've had an interesting life," said one of the interns "It kind of makes my Netflix after work seem pretty dry."

As the summer unfolded Paul was given the task to prepare and deliver several Lunch and Learn presentations around his career challenges and career successes. The interns admitted that they learned much from Paul's work and life experiences and discovered that they were very similar in that they too shared a strong drive to succeed.

Ambition had recognized itself—they all had it! One of the interns shared they all couldn't be more different than Paul in gender, nationality, age, or experiences. On the outside they seemed to have nothing in common… but inside they were very similar and that they too had a lot of ambition and drive.

Paul's understanding and respect for the Millennial interns also grew as did his knowledge of PowerPoint, social media, technology, how to take iPhone photos, and the "manbun." The intern program was a huge success and word has it that an 80-year-old executive is looking to take Paul's place next summer!

"Calling out around the world,
Are you ready for a brand new beat?
Summer's here and the time is right
For dancing in the street.
They're dancing in Chicago,
Down in New Orleans,
In New York City
All we need is music, sweet music
There'll be music everywhere
There'll be swinging and swaying and records playing,
Dancing in the street
Oh, it doesn't matter what you wear,
Just as long as you are there
So come on, every guy, grab a girl
Everywhere around the world
They'll be dancing
They're dancing in the street
It's an invitation across the nation,
A chance for folks to meet
There'll be laughing, singing, and music swinging,
Dancing in the street"

Lyrics from
"Dancing in the Street"
by Marvin Gaye 1964
Sung by Martha and the Vandellas

Is There a Little Baby Boomer in You?

- ☐ My career defines me and my work is my "badge of honor."
- ☐ I am always willing to take on more responsibility.
- ☐ I have been known to spend now and worry later.
- ☐ I live to work and look for extra projects in my free time.
- ☐ I use social media, search engines, smartphones, and other digital devices to search for information and stay in touch with family and friends.
- ☐ I find that I would rather do things myself than ask others for help, mostly because I want it done right the first time.
- ☐ I have been known to challenge authority and the status quo.
- ☐ I keep up with current trends and want to stay relevant.
- ☐ I admit I love Facebook and post lots of family photos.
- ☐ I respond well to attention and recognition, but I don't take criticism well.
- ☐ Respect is something I believe we could all use a little more of when it comes to our leaders, police, teachers, and elders.

Who Is the Baby Boomer?

Born 1946 – 1963

Babies Galore!

The name "Baby Boomer" refers to the tremendous spike in births when WWII came to an end. In fact, the birth of the Boomers signaled the end of 16 years of depression and war. But now as peace and prosperity returned, America was ready for a new start.

The post-war era brought not only babies, but also a new confidence in the economy. Corporations began to grow larger and more profitable, and labor unions were in their heyday promising higher wages, benefits, and a brighter future for their members. Parents of this new generation wanted to give their children so many of the opportunities and things they did not have in their own childhoods.

Lifestyle Changes and the Women's Movement

One of the first lifestyle changes after the war was the birth of "the burbs." Visionary developers bought land on the outskirts of cities and built mass-produced homes (tract homes) on the land. Low interest rates through the G.I. Bill for vets tempted many city dwellers to move out to the burbs, while others just wanted to leave the city life and raise their families in a safer environment.

Although the flight from cities to suburbs was great for family life, many women felt isolated and trapped away from their city lifestyle. Another point to remember is that during the war some 350,000 women served in the U.S. Armed Forces, both at home and abroad. More than 310,000 women worked in the U.S. aircraft industry in 1943, representing 65 percent of the industry's total workforce (compared to just one percent in the pre-war years). Rosie the Riveter symbolized the newfound strength of the working woman during the war years.

However, in the 1950s, a shift in thinking was on the rise, and women were told to go back into the home, where their most important job was to bear and rear children, along with being a good wife who knew how to cook and keep a tidy home. For some women, this shift in lifestyle and values generated a huge dissatisfaction, and the women's liberation movement began contributing to the feminist movement of the 1960s.

Television, Credit Cards, and Consumerism

The post-war economy was able to raise the standard of living for many families. Moving from apartment living to a home with a "family room" required more furniture! A new concept in buying with a credit card was born, and people began purchasing products on credit, revving up the economy: televisions, Hi-Fi systems, new cars, and clothing. Consumerism wasn't just for the adults as marketers begin to realize there were huge profits to be made from the Boomer babies too. They began to watch the habits of the newest generation, who were now watching TV and, in particular, Walt Disney's Mickey Mouse Club. Boomer children begged their parents to buy them mouse ears, Davey Crocket hats, Hula-Hoops, Frisbees, and lots of other toys now being advertised on TV. The Boomer child had buying power! This new affluent spending may have been the precursor to the Boomers' philosophy of spend-now-and-worry-later lifestyle.

The Counterculture of the Sixties

The first Boomers entered their teens and said "so long" to Elvis and "hello" to the Beatles, the Rolling Stones, and the Dave Clark Five. Bob Dylan sang "The Times They Are A-Changin'" as civil unrest exploded with the Vietnam War, and many Baby Boomers began to gravitate to a counterculture. Rejecting the status quo, student activism appeared on many college campuses. Young adults became activists protesting for civil rights and against the war.

Other Boomers dropped out completely and they were called hippies. The hippie arrived on the scene with long hair, Birkenstocks, tie-dyed clothing, peace signs, and hallucinogenic drugs.

Living the American Dream Requires "Work, Work, and More Work"

When the oldest Boomers entered the workforce in the late 60s and early 70s, they brought with them their vision of the American Dream, a competitive nature, a strong need to be seen as an individual, and a new style of leadership. They replaced their predecessors' "my way or the highway" style with a more democratic consensus of leadership and teamwork.

Their dream was challenged early on. The 1970–1980 decade was filled with uncertainty in the U.S. workforce. The U.S. was moving from a manufacturing economy to a service economy, and the transition involved downsizings, mergers, and reorganizations. Attitudes towards work and the employer were changing. As the uncertainty grew, some Boomers felt betrayed, but they continued to work longer and harder. Boomers have felt they are hardwired for work. As Boomers have aged, they also have admitted that they have stayed in jobs that had no growth or future, but still continued to work hard calling their work a "badge of honor."

In 1991, we signed the North American Trade Agreement, and many U.S. manufacturing companies moved to Mexico and overseas. The look and feel of work was changing and many Boomers moved into management.

Today, the oldest Baby Boomers are already in their 70s. By 2030, about one in five Americans will be older than 65, and some experts believe that the aging of the population will place a strain on social welfare systems.

Bill Clinton was the first Baby Boomer to serve as president, followed by George W. Bush, Barack Obama, and Donald Trump. Baby Boomers have risen to the highest levels of corporations and elected offices. Their time is now fading into the golden years of retirement, but they have left an enduring mark on our society.

"I can't get no, oh, no, no, no, hey, hey, hey
That's what I say
I can't get no satisfaction, I can't get no satisfaction
'Cause I try and I try and I try and I try
I can't get no, I can't get no"

Lyrics from "Satisfaction"
by Mick Jagger and Keith Richards
Sung by The Rolling Stones – 1965

Boomer Values

Our values are formed early in our lives and from the earliest days, starting in kindergarten and all the way through to our adulthood. For the Boomers, they learned early on that in order to be noticed and achieve, they had to compete for attention, resources, and success. So, it is natural that for so many Boomers, competitiveness feels like it is part of their DNA.

Today as Boomers age, they are taking their values with them into retirement. They keep on pushing, exhibiting their hard working dedicated style in their volunteer endeavors, community involvement, exercise programs, and their interest in their grandchildren.

Boomers Value

- *Achievement/Success/Ambition*
- *Commitment*
- *Independence*
- *Goals*
- *Family*
- *Dignity*
- *Drive*
- *Responsibility*
- *Individual choice*
- *Health and wellness*
- *Personal growth/Fulfillment/Gratification*
- *Youthfulness*
- *Self-Actualization*

Key Attributes of Baby Boomers

- *Adaptive*
- *Optimistic*
- *Determined*
- *Goal-oriented*
- *Desires personal growth*
- *Self-Improvement*
- *Focus on individual choices and freedom*
- *Adaptive to a diverse workplace*
- *Positive attitude*
- *Self Absorption...admit it Boomers!*

Boomers are Influenced by

- *Television*
- *The Beatles and music*
- *The Vietnam War*
- *Hippies/Woodstock/Freedom*
- *Civil Rights*
- *Women's Movement*
- *Sexual Revolution*
- *Cold War*
- *Space Travel*
- *NAFTA*

Movies that Define the Boomers

- *The Graduate*
- *The Big Chill*
- *Easy Rider*
- *The Godfather (all of them)*
- *Annie Hall*
- *Apocalypse Now*

- *Kramer vs. Kramer*
- *Mr. Mom*
- *Baby Boom*
- *Bob, Carol, Ted and Alice*
- *The Way We Were*
- *Up in the Air*
- *Breakfast at Tiffany's*
- *Woman of the Year*
- *The Devil Wears Prada*
- *The Incredibles*
- *Working Girl*
- *Network*
- *Nine to Five*
- *Sense and Sensibility*

Boomers Who Rock

- *Bruce Springsteen*
- *Billy Joel*
- *John Travolta*
- *Robert Plant*
- *Elton John*
- *Stevie Nix*
- *Madonna*
- *Sheryl Crow*
- *Huey Lewis*
- *Tom Petty*
- *Steven Tyler*
- *Elton John*
- *Barry Gibb*
- *Jon Bon Jovi*
- *Axl Rose*
- *Gene Simmons*
- *John Mellencamp*
- *Alan Jackson*
- *Dolly Parton*
- *Whitney Houston*

What the Boomers Want Today

- *Respect from younger workers, children and grandchildren*
- *To find a flexible route to retirement*
- *Willingness to take risks*
- *Work efficiently*
- *Honoring their decisions*
- *Individual choice in care, housing, and lifestyle*
- *Freedom*
- *Security*
- *Health and a sense of well-being*

A Closer Look at a Boomer who Rocks

Desiree Rumbaugh

My daughter, Meredith (Generation X), became interested in yoga when she was in graduate school. Now, in addition to her "daytime career" as a government consultant, she is passionate about teaching yoga, and she still continues her training with some fantastic yogis.

One of her first teachers is a remarkable woman, whose name is Desiree Rumbaugh. Meredith's enthusiasm prompted me to begin taking some yoga classes to help ease the pain in my stiff knees, and she sent me a therapeutic yoga DVD by, you guessed it, Desiree Rumbaugh. So, my journey began. I started going to yoga classes, and in the evenings, I did my home DVD practice with Desiree—and as a result my knees started feeling better!

I was a year into my practice of yoga when Meredith suggested we meet in Boston and drive up to Kripalu in The Berkshires to take a weekend workshop with Desiree. I agreed, but I was fearful since I was only a beginner.

Kripalu is fantastic (please check it out at kripalu.org), and the workshop was as great as it was challenging. I loved all of it...and Desiree too. That weekend I gained a new perspective on my body, aging, and living a vibrant life.

At the time, Desiree had just turned 50, and she shared with us her fantastic vision of a yoga class designed for over-50 yogis called "Wisdom Warriors", which combined the "wisdom" of getting older with the "warrior" of toughing it out! Desiree shared that her goal is to help people over 50 to continue to have a friendly and somewhat functional relationship with their bodies—keeping them strong, safe, and vibrant.

That workshop took place in July of 2012. Today, the Wisdom Warriors are thriving! The classes are filled with Boomers (and some Traditionalists) who still want to pursue the thrill of learning new poses and trying new and challenging things, yet are safe in their practice. Wisdom Warriors don't give up, they show up! Warriors work with what they have, and sometimes they have injuries and pain—but they still show up!

As we age, our bodies change. For some people a sadness or loss of spirit enters as they discover that they are losing strength, balance, and the ability to do more. As we enter mid-life, our joints stiffen, our bones weaken, and for some our mental acuity lessens. This feeling of sadness is a natural result for most Boomers who were the most active generation in history. The generations before the Boomers were told to adjust to aging by slowing down, taking it easy, resting, and not pushing so hard, but the Boomers don't want to follow that advice.

Desiree has a different perspective on aging. She encourages both men and women to be fearless and to celebrate being an over-50 Warrior, encouraging all generations to discover how to live their best life possible. She says in her book, *Fearless at Fifty*, that pain is like a doorbell...and when it rings, we need to answer it. She says pain, injury, and illness should not be ignored. The real problem is when we pretend that it does not exist. According to Desiree, "When the going gets tough, the tough have to heal."

We have to listen to what our bodies are telling us, and practicing yoga helps us live a preventative life. When we pursue yoga on a regular basis, we become more sensitive and tuned in to our bodies.

Desiree is a Boomer who has rocked my world. She has helped me become fearless through practicing yoga. I try to make time every day for yoga, and I try to push myself in the right way to find teachers who keep me and my body safe. I feel stronger now than I felt 10 years ago, but the best part of it is that I listen to my body, and it guides me to the work I can do each day.

Desiree has recently co-authored with Michelle Marchildon *Fearless After Fifty – How to Thrive with Grace, Grit and Yoga.* This book rocks!

"If I had $1000000 I'd buy you a house
If I had $1000000 I'd buy you furniture for your house
(Maybe a nice chesterfield or an ottoman)
If I had $1000000 I'd buy you a K-Car
(a nice Reliant automobile)
If I had $1000000 I'd buy your love

If I had $1000000 I'd build a tree fort in our yard
If I had $1000000 You could help, it wouldn't be that hard
If I had $1000000

Maybe we could put a little tiny fridge in there somewhere
([Talking:] We could just go up there and hang out.
Like open the fridge and stuff, and there'd be foods laid out for us
With little pre-wrapped sausages and things. Mmmmm.
They have pre-wrapped sausages but
they don't have pre-wrapped bacon.
Well can you blame them. Yeah)

If I had $1000000 I'd buy you a fur coat
(but not a real fur coat—that's cruel)
If I had $1000000 I'd buy you an exotic pet
(Like a llama or an emu)
If I had $1000000 I'd buy you John Merrick's remains
(All them crazy elephant bones)
If I had $1000000 I'd buy your love"

Lyrics from "If I Had a $1,000,000"
by Steven Page and Ed Robinson
Sung by the Bare Naked Ladies – 1992

Is There a Little Gen X in You?

- ☐ I am a self-starter, and I am willing to work hard when I see that it's necessary, but don't interrupt me when I am focused.

- ☐ "I work to live." It is my life—not my work—that defines me. My work is a means to an end.

- ☐ I am a saver and I save for the future.

- ☐ I enjoy doing Do-It-Yourself (DIY) projects in my free time.

- ☐ I use social media to engage with my friends, and I value their reviews and suggestions.

- ☐ I find that I would rather work on my own and that means where I want and when I want. I love the idea of telecommuting.

- ☐ I have been known to be direct and even abrupt. I can't tolerate BS.

- ☐ I keep my personal life separate from my work life when possible.

- ☐ I admit I am a little overprotective of my kids—it's a scary world out there—and, yeah, I've heard that term "helicopter parent."

- ☐ Respect is something I believe we could all use a little more of when it comes to our leaders, police, teachers, and elders.

Who Is Generation X?

Born 1964 – 1980

X Marks the Spot

The generation following the Boomers is known as Generation X or Gen X. In numbers, Gen Xers (51 million people) is the smallest generation. It is sandwiched between the two largest groups—the Boomers (75 million) and the Millennials (78 million).

Gen X children were born during a time of shifting social and family values, a challenging economy, and advances in technology in the U.S.

They were the children of the Boomers—the "Me Generation"—who were deep into self-actualizing. As parents, the Boomers seemed to focus less on their children and more on themselves and their careers, and this impacted how Gen X kids grew up.

The generic label "generation X" has been used at various times throughout history to refer to populations of alienated youth, but in 1991 Douglas Coupland coined the term, specifically referring to the youth of this time period. In his book *Generation X: Tales for an Accelerated Culture*, the letter "X" was meant to signify the generation's random, ambiguous, and contradictory ways.

Does the name Generation X sound a bit negative? As Coupland put it, "Negative? Moi? I think realistic might be a better word." Yes, Generation X—the name really seemed to fit this new generation, and the name stuck.

Changing Economy, Changing Families

Gen X kids grew up in harder times than the Boomers did. Between 1979 and 1995, some 43 million jobs were lost through corporate downsizing. Newly created jobs paid less and offered fewer benefits, and stagflation appeared. In economics, stagflation happens when the inflation rate is high, the economic growth rate slows, and unemployment remains steadily high.

Many families needed more than one income to survive and women reentered the workforce to provide the extra income.

The challenges in the American economy combined with other social changes—including the availability of birth control (specifically the pill), feminism, increased levels of education among women and men—meant big changes for the American family.

A new trend was occurring: American couples began to marry later, have fewer children, and divorce more frequently. In 1973, when "the Pill" went on the market, most Americans lived in nuclear-style families. The average married couple had three to four children, and mothers stayed home and tended to the family.

By 2000, the average family had shrunk to two children (one of the reasons that this generation is so small), and one out of two marriages ended in divorce. Almost a third of American children were being raised by a single parent or an unmarried couple—further contributing to profound changes in family dynamics.

Growing Up in the 70s and 80s

Freedom! Well sort of...kids had lots of freedom back in the 70s and 80s. They played outside. They had wheels—their bikes—and they got to roam and ride all day until the streetlights came on at night.

But even when they weren't playing, Gen X children were often left on their own. The term "Latchkey Kids," a name created by Boomers, referred to children who came home from school to an empty house because mom was working. The kids of this era were given a great deal of responsibility and a list of chores was often left on the kitchen table to be completed before mom got home: empty the dishwasher, plug in the crock pot, do your homework, and help your brother and sister with theirs, fill the ice cube trays, set the table, and don't make a mess.

For all the talk about this lost, "slacker" generation, most Gen Xers grew up fast and learned responsibility early. They did get many of the items on the list done... but only after hours of watching music videos (the rise of MTV), listening to the radio, and making mixtapes to share with their friends.

Now let's pause for a moment. If you were born between 1965 and 1979 and your mom did not work and you did not have lots of independence, you may be more like a Boomer than a Gen Xer. The same goes for Boomers—no matter what your age, if your mom worked and you were left alone to be independent and more personally responsible, you may relate more to Gen X.

From a parenting and educating perspective, this was not a "coddled" generation. Gen X kids saw firsthand that their parents were human and fallible, and they often found themselves giving their parents advice and comfort. Autonomy and self-reliance, rather than respect for authority, were natural byproducts of the Generation X childhood.

More than likely, this incarnation of childhood freedom (and adolescent responsibility) will never happen again, and growing up in this environment has shaped the adults that Gen Xers have become.

Reality Bites

Gen X children grew up watching their world become a scarier place. Gen Xers saw pictures of lost children on milk cartons and were the first generation that needed to take their Halloween candy to the hospital to get it x-rayed because a neighbor may have slipped a razor blade or pins into the Milk Duds.

They learned about stranger danger (red light!) and watched on TV as a frying pan came on the screen and heard a voice announce: "This is your brain," and then an egg was cracked into a pan with the voice explaining, "This is your brain on drugs!"

They also grew up in an era when many of the sacred institutions (churches, schools, government) fell apart or let them down. Gen Xers saw corporations like Enron and WorldCom crumble, leaving employees with empty pension funds. They watched in real time as the doomed Challenger exploded, and as Heisman winner O.J. Simpson crouched in the back of his white Bronco while his friend drove it down a Los Angeles freeway.

Is it any wonder that this generation is known for being intensely cynical? Here are just a few dates of the memorable events that squelched their ability to blindly trust and further contribute to their skeptical nature:

1972 – Watergate scandal
1973 – Energy Crisis and Long Gas Lines
1979 – Three Mile Island Meltdown
1980s – Priest, Politician, and Teacher scandals
1986 – Challenger Disaster
1990s – Corporate Layoffs (parents laid off)
1992 – Rodney King Beating/Police Brutality
1995 – Clinton-Lewinsky scandal
2001 – Enron/Tyco corporate scandal

Gen X: There Will Never be Another!

As parenting styles have changed—both as a response to living in a "scarier" world and to counter the hands-off approach that defined the typical Gen X childhood—children today stay a little closer to home, under the watchful eyes of their grownups.

Looking back at this generation, it's easy to see that Gen X could possibly be the last generation of children and teens to grow up with freedom, independence, and the luxury to try different things on their own, fail, and try again.

Generation X Values

Research tells us that the time between 8 years old and 13 years old is called the modeling period in a child's life, when children are impressed with the outside world. Here, the shift is from the parent to what is happening on

TV: evening news, local as well as world events are now coming into the picture. In the lifetime of Generation X, the world was changing.

As described above, when most Gen Xers entered these modeling years they saw a troubled economy, the first "lay offs" were happening in the US, and many of the leaders and institutions were failing them.

If you ask a Gen Xer what they remember most about the world they grew up in, they may answer "the Challenger Disaster." Most Gen Xers were sitting in a classroom with their teachers and classmates watching in real time as seven astronauts (one a school teacher) died when the Space Shuttle Challenger exploded on screen! This event made a huge imprint—adding that yet another institution failed.

Gen Xers Value

- *Working to live*
- *Fiscal conservatism*
- *Dedication to family*
- *Relationships*
- *Responsibility*
- *Freedom*
- *Autonomy*
- *Authenticity*
- *Mission/Meaningful work*

Key Attributes of Generation X

- *Adaptive*
- *Independent*
- *Highly self-reliant*
- *Determined*

- *Dedicated parents*
- *Understanding of money*
- *Strong survival skills*
- *Goal-oriented*
- *Desire personal growth*
- *Self-improvement*
- *Skeptical*
- *Focus on individual choices and freedom*
- *Adaptive to a diverse workplace*

Gen Xers are Influenced by

- *Fall of the Berlin Wall*
- *Challenger disaster*
- *Moscow 1980 Olympics boycott*
- *Working mothers*
- *Dungeons and Dragons*
- *Personal computers*
- *The Internet*
- *Operation Desert Storm*
- *Family TV time & Saturday morning cartoons*

Movies that Define Gen X

- *Reality Bites*
- *Clerks*
- *Slacker*
- *The Breakfast Club* *(ok, anything by John Hughes)*
- *Pretty in Pink*
- *Sixteen Candles*
- *Ferris Bueller's Day Off*
- *Singles*
- *Swingers*
- *Say Anything* *(Lloyd Dobler!!)*
- *Better off Dead* *(I want my two dollars!)*
- *Grosse Pointe Blank*
- *The Princess Bride*
- *The Lost Boys*
- *Weird Science*
- *Pump Up the Volume*
- *Dirty Dancing*
- *Goodfellas*
- *The Karate Kid*
- *Stand by Me*
- *Goonies*
- *Back to the Future*
- *ET*
- *Footloose*
- *Guardians of the Galaxy*
- *And on TV...Stranger Things* *(This may have come out in 2016, but it nails what it was like to grow up as an Xer...strange things aside, of course.)*

Gen Xers Who Rock

- *Bono*
- *50 Cent*
- *John Mayer*
- *Jay Z*
- *Kanye West*
- *Snoop Dog*
- *Jimmy Fallon*
- *Janet Jackson*
- *Dave Matthews*
- *Gwen Stefani*
- *Blake Shelton*
- *Adam Levine*
- *Usher*
- *Rivers Cuomo*
- *Chris Martin*
- *Kenny Chesney*
- *Faith Hill*
- *Tim McGraw*
- *Lenny Kravitz*
- *Billie Joe Armstrong*
- *Mariah Carey*
- *Mary Jane Blige*

"Never confuse having a career with having a life"

Eddie Bauer
shopping bag slogan

What Generation X Wants Today!

- *Time with their families*
- *Flexibility*
- *Career advancement*
- *Honest feedback*
- *Freedom*
- *Options*
- *Functional, positive, fun work environment*
- *Access to information*
- *Access to leadership*

"Oh
Once upon a midnight dreary
I woke with something in my head
I couldn't escape the memory
Of a phone call and of what you said

Like a game show contestant with a parting gift
I could not believe my eyes
When I saw through the voice of a trusted friend
Who needs to humor me and tell me lies
Yeah, humor me and tell me lies

And I'll lie too and say I don't mind
And as we seek so shall we find
And when you're feeling open I'll still be here
But not without a certain degree of fear
Of what will be with you and me
I still can see things hopefully
But you
Why you wanna give me a run-around
Is it a sure-fire way to speed things up
When all it does is slow me down"

Lyrics from "Run-Around"
by John C. Popper
Sung by The Blues Traveler – 1994

A Gen Xer Who Rocks

Tina Fey

They say that the youngest in the family is "the funny one" and that was surely the case in my family growing up. My sisters were eight and eleven years older than me and my role was to make the family laugh. So I naturally watched a lot of funny sitcoms, and when I could stay up to watch Johnny Carson, I got to see a lot of comedians.

I laughed at *I Love Lucy* and I enjoyed the *Mary Tyler Moore Show*, but *The Carol Burnett Show* was not one of my faves (don't hate me, please). Joan Rivers made me gasp, George Carlin talked about his stuff, and Richard Pryor was funny and scary at the same time. I really love Eddie Izzard, Eddie Murphy, Seinfeld, Ellen, and the list goes on and on to include Chris Rock, Dave Chappelle, and Louis CK—all are gut laugh-inducing.

But my all-time favorite, the one that rocks my world and inspires me to find the humor in life and to do more creative work, is Gen Xer Tina Fey.

I have always been a fan, but I got to know Tina better after reading her book *Bossy Pants*. Her mix of Gen X humor with a sting, a little self-deprecation, and a lot of introspection, kept me totally engaged. Her book is a memoir about a funny, nerdy, not-so-pretty Gen X girl (born in 1970 into a "normal" family), who takes an interesting journey into the comedy business.

To me, Tina Fay is the poster child for Gen Xers.

Starting with her work ethic—Tina makes hard work and perseverance shine through—she studied and performed improv at The Second City in Chicago.

There she worked with people like Amy Poehler, Steve Carrell, Rachel Dratch, Neil Flynn, Tim Meadows, Amy Sederis, and Stephen Colbert. In her book she says that working at Second City set her on a career path to *Saturday Night Live (SNL)*.

She then joined *SNL* (stayed for nine years—no job-hopping here) as a writer, and later became head writer and a performer. She was known for her position as co-anchor in the Weekend Update segment with Jimmy Fallon.

In 2004 she co-starred in and wrote the screenplay for *Mean Girls*, which I hear is one of the Millennials' favorite movies.

She left *SNL* in 2006 and created the television series *30 Rock*, where she played Liz Lemon, the head writer of a fictional sketch comedy series. Liz Lemon made nerddom cool—"By the hammer of Thor, I'm running late!"

Later, Tina starred in the comedy films *Baby Mama, Date Night, Megamind, Sisters*, and *Whiskey Tango Foxtrot.*

In 2015 she created and produced the Netflix comedy hit *Unbreakable Kimmy Schmidt.*

She is also a wife and a mother of two daughters—having baby number 2 in her 40s—so Gen X!

What I love most is how she downplays her physical appearance with a little self-deprecation, constantly reminding us that our culture places too much importance on how a woman looks. She makes this point in the character of Liz Lemon in *30 Rock* and in these comments:

"It's hard to be a woman."

"Steve Carell's *Foxcatcher* look took two hours to put on, including his hairstyling and makeup. Just for comparison, it took me three hours today to prepare for my role as 'human woman.'"

At the Golden Globes, Tina and Amy rocked it as hosts for three years! They always get across their perspective on gender equality through humor.

On Hollywood ageism, they pointed to Patricia Arquette, 46, who played her role in *Boyhood* over a 12-year period, and said, "*Boyhood* proves that there are still roles for women over 40, as long as you're hired while you're still under 40."

Another ageism dig was "*Gravity* is nominated for best film. It's the story of how George Clooney would rather float away into space and die than spend one more minute with a woman his own age."

Finally, in *Bossy Pants*, Tina tells women to trust their instincts and just do your jobs the best way you know how, not caring what others think!

"I wanna be a billionaire so freakin' bad
Buy all of the things I never had
Uh, I wanna be on the cover of Forbes magazine
Smiling next to Oprah and the Queen

Oh every time I close my eyes I see my name in shining lights
Yeah, a different city every night oh right
I swear the world better prepare For when I'm a billionaire

Yeah I would have a show like Oprah
I would be the host of, everyday Christmas
Give Travie a wish list
I'd probably pull an Angelina and Brad Pitt
And adopt a bunch of babies that ain't never had shit
Give away a few Mercedes like here lady have this
And last but not least grant somebody their last wish

It's been a couple months that I've been single so
You can call me Travie Claus minus the Ho Ho
Get it, hehe, I'd probably visit where Katrina hit
And damn sure do a lot more than FEMA did

Yeah can't forget about me stupid
Everywhere I go Imma have my own theme music
Oh every time I close my eyes I see my name in shining lights
A different city every night oh right
I swear the world better prepare For when I'm a billionaire
Oh ooh oh ooh for when I'm a billionaire
Oh ooh oh ooh for when I'm a billionaire"

Lyrics from "I Wanna Be a Billionaire"
Written by Philip Lawrence, Ari Levine,
Bruno Mars, and Travis McCoy
Sung by Bruno Mars – 2010

Is There a Little Millennial in You?

- ☐ I am not content with the status quo. I think of how things can be better. I am curious, and open to new ideas.
- ☐ I embrace change and see change as an opportunity to grow.
- ☐ I think of technology as a tool to engage with others and increase my productivity.
- ☐ I am not fond of long hours behind a desk when the work can be done anywhere.
- ☐ I am motivated by humanitarian causes.
- ☐ I am known as a self-promoter and have an opportunist's mindset—I know how to grow my personal brand.
- ☐ I have a low B.S. tolerance and I seek out those people who are authentically themselves.
- ☐ I crave feedback and want to grow, learn and advance as quickly as possible.
- ☐ I am impatient!

Who Is the Millennial?

Born 1981 – 2001

Baby on Board!

Millennials, also known as Generation Y, Gen Y, Echo Boomers, are the children of Baby Boomers and older Gen Xers.

The Millennial generation is the largest generation in US history and across the entire world. Because of this, their impact on the global economy is going to be enormous.

Growing Up Millennial

Millennials arrived on the scene when the attitudes about child rearing were about to change. The Boomers were raised with the "Children should be seen and not heard" mindset. Gen Xers were raised with an independent style where busy parents told the kids to "grow up" "stay outside until the street lights come on."

In the mid 1980s America became more child-centric—a shift was happening! Across the globe, parents worried about the children being "safe," became overprotective, and the freedom experienced

"You've got a friend in me
You've got a friend in me
When the road looks rough ahead
And you're miles and miles
From your nice warm bed
You just remember what your old pal said
Boy, you've got a friend in me
Yeah, you've got a friend in me"

Lyrics from "You've Got a Friend in Me"
by Randy Newman
Sung by Randy Newman in Toy Story – 1995

by Gen X vanished. The metal playground equipment of the 1960s and 1970s (jungle gyms, monkey bars, and merry-go-rounds) vanished and safer, softer playgrounds appeared.

Parents scheduled their kids in activities, protected them from dangers (both real and exaggerated), and continually praised them to build their self-esteem.

Millennials are the first generation to really "like" their parents. For Millennials, the days of spankings disappeared, replaced with new techniques for "respectful parenting."

Many Millennials see their parents as friends—even best friends—and often involve their parents in both life and work-related decisions.

On April 19, 1995, when the oldest Millennials were 15, a truck-bomb exploded outside the Alfred P. Murrah Federal Building in Oklahoma City, Oklahoma, leaving

168 people dead and hundreds more injured. Four years later was Columbine, and then, just two years later, 9-11. These acts, along with natural disasters such as the Tsunami in Asia and Hurricane Katrina, turned our focus inward with a deep desire to protect home and family. Millennials were the first generation, but not the last, raised in this new protected environment.

Time to Grow Up!

Millennials are not in a rush to move out of their parents' homes, buy cars, get married, have children, and purchase homes. Ever wonder why?

While every generation has struggled to find their professional path and develop their personal and financial independence as they establish a life for themselves, Millennials are the first generation to come of age during a time of technological changes, globalization, and the 2008 economic disruption. This gives them a different set of behaviors, perspectives, and experiences than previous generations.

The 2008-09 Great Recession lasted through 2015 and took its toll on the Millennials entering the workforce. Many could not find employment, others were let go because they were the last to be hired. The struggle was real!

If you stop and think about it, the recession may have played a big part in:

- *Millennials moving back in with their parents after graduation.*
- *Millennials not making large purchases such as cars and homes.*
- *Millennials postponing marriage and children.*

Digital Natives

I remember listening to a speaker named Marc Prensky who first use the term, "digital natives." He called the children born after 1981 this term, referring to the fact that they were the first generation to grow up with tools such as the home computer, the Internet, cell phones, video games, and MP3 players.

The "digital native" was born with technology in their hands, unlike those born before the technology, who he calls the digital immigrants. In the early days of the tech revolution, the digital immigrants (myself included) printed out documents, had training on how to use computers and read programs, read manuals, and the list goes on and on.

Today technology is an integral part of all of our lives. It is an everyday occurrence to see two- and three-year-olds on cell phones and iPads swiping, learning, and laughing. Millennials are at the forefront of this integration, and as the first generation of "digital natives," their affinity for technology is shaping how they watch, listen, and shop.

Millennial Values

As with Generation X, the way that Millennials experienced the world in the modeling period of their lives (ages 8-13) impacted the way that Millennial adults respond to their world. Changes in parenting, in technology, and in the world have contributed to what Millennials value.

In addition, Millennials' attitude toward ownership is different from the other generations, introducing us to the concept of a "sharing economy"—Uber anyone?

Millennials also care about their bodies and what they put into them. Their active and healthy lifestyle influences trends not only in food and drink but also in the world of fashion.

But maybe most importantly, Millennials are dedicated to making the world a better place.

Millennials Value

- *Individuality*
- *Purpose*
- *Doing good*
- *Sharing (i.e., the sharing economy)*
- *Independence*
- *"The Experience"*
- *Family*
- *Friends*
- *Diversity*
- *Collaboration*
- *Individual choice*
- *Health and wellness*

Key Attributes of Millennials

- *Best educated of all generations—so far*
- *Independent, yet team player*
- *Optimistic*
- *Ambitious*
- *Open to new ideas*
- *Social*
- *Tech Savvy/Digital Generation*
- *Innovative*
- *Adaptive to a diverse workplace*
- *Positive attitude*

- *Self-absorbed*
- *Strong sense of entitlement*

Millennials are Influenced by

- *Digital media*
- *Child-focused parenting*
- *School shootings*
- *Video games*
- *Computers*
- *Google*
- *Amazon*
- *Social media*
- *Apple IPod, IPhone*
- *AIDS*
- *Terrorism*
- *Internet*

Movies that Define Millennials

- *Lion King*
- *Toy Story*
- *The Lord of the Rings*
- *Harry Potter*
- *Napoleon Dynamite*
- *Mean Girls*
- *Titanic*
- *Hunger Games*
- *Legally Blonde*
- *Fight Club*
- *Remember the Titans*
- *Garden State*
- *Juno*
- *Slumdog Millionaire*

- *Fast and Furious*
- *The Hangover*
- *The Social Network*
- *Knocked Up*
- *Bridesmaids*
- *Catfish*
- *Twilight*
- *Spiderman*

Millennials who Rock

- *Bruno Mars*
- *Katy Perry*
- *Britney Spears*
- *Alicia Keys*
- *Michelle Branch*
- *Justin Timberlake*
- *Beyoncé*
- *Justin Bieber*
- *Selena Gomez*
- *Ed Sheeran*
- *Miranda Lambert*
- *Drake*
- *Rihanna*
- *2Pac*
- *Eric Church*
- *Chris Brown*
- *Lady Gaga*
- *Miley Cyrus*
- *Adam Lambert*

"Hey, I was doing just fine before I met you
I drink too much and that's an issue but I'm okay

Hey, you tell your friends it was nice to meet them
But I hope I never see them again

I know it breaks your heart
Moved to the city in a broke down car
And four years, no calls
Now you're looking pretty in a hotel bar

And I can't stop
No, I can't stop

So baby pull me closer in the backseat of your Rover
That I know you can't afford
Bite that tattoo on your shoulder
Pull the sheets right off the corner
Of the mattress that you stole
From your roommate back in Boulder

We ain't ever getting older
We ain't ever getting older
We ain't ever getting older"

Lyrics from "Closer"
by Andrew Taggart, Ashley Frangipane, Shaun Frank,
Freddy Kennett, Isaac Slade & Joe King
Sung by The Chainsmokers – 2016

A Closer Look at Millennials Who Rock

Brian and Joe (the Airbnb guys)

In March of 2013, I wanted to visit my daughter, her husband, and their new baby. The problem was their small apartment in the Adams Morgan area of D.C. had no extra room for a guest. Meredith suggested that I get an Airbnb nearby. I had heard of Airbnb and I really wanted to see the baby, so I agreed. (Actually, I didn't want to use Airbnb. I thought it was kind of creepy staying in someone's apartment, but I pushed through and did it!) It wasn't so bad!

Today, Airbnb is valued at over $25.5 billion.

Here's the Story:

Brian Chesky (b. August 29, 1981) and Joe Gebbia (b. August 21, 1981) were friends and classmates at Rhode Island School of Design. Both guys were studying industrial design and both knew that they were meant to be entrepreneurs and would someday go into business together. Upon graduation Brian moved to Los Angeles and Joe to San Francisco where he was hired as an industrial design engineer. Joe moved into a pretty cool apartment in San Francisco, and he encouraged Brian to move to San Francisco and be his roommate. Joe wanted to take the plunge with Brian to go into some sort of business together, so he quit his day job. Ironically, just about when Brian was unpacking, the rent on Joe's apartment skyrocketed and they couldn't afford the apartment.

These were two creative guys, and they had to come up with a plan to get more cash. It just so happened on that weekend there was a huge conference in San Francisco (a design conference), and there were no hotel rooms in the entire city. They got the crazy idea to rent out their apartment living room space. They bought three air mattresses and decided to charge $80 a night for each mattress and serve the guests a homemade breakfast in the morning (that was the easy part).

The big question was how would they get the three guests? They could post it on Craig's List—that would be the easiest—a no brainer. But on second thought, they discussed that these people would be sleeping in their living room. They needed to know who they were and a way to check them out! And they needed to take the time to build a website with photos of the space. Luckily for them, they had not only the talent but also the drive to create their own website since they really did have an entrepreneurial mindset. These two were very resourceful! Bam, it was up the next day. "Airbed and Breakfast" was ready for business. But now they had another challenge. How were they going to get the word out?

They realized that they had to be marketers, and they emailed every design blogger on their radar, telling them about Airbed and Breakfast (highlighting the air mattress idea). To their surprise, they got a lot of responses from all over the world, which opened their eyes to the possibility that this could work—everywhere!

So they got their first three guests for the upcoming weekend. Before I go on, think about what kinds of people would want to sleep on an air mattress in some stranger's living room with other strangers. Young, broke guys, right? Wrong. The three people that slept that first night on the air mattresses in Joe's and Brian's living room were professionals all over the age of 30.

The greatest thing about the three strangers who became Joe's and Brian's inspiration was that they shared their stories along with some new and great ideas and encouraged the guys to keep going. That weekend they made enough money to pay the rent, and they began their wild journey to creating one of the biggest disruptors in the travel business.

Read the rest of the story in Leigh Gallagher's book *The Airbnb Story: How Three Ordinary Guys Disrupted an Industry, Made Billions...and Created Plenty of Controversy.*

"People are people so why should it be
You and I should get along so awfully
So we're different colours
And we're different creeds
And different people have different needs
It's obvious you hate me
Though I've done nothing wrong
I never even met you
So what could I have done"

Lyrics from "People are People"
by Martin Gore
Sung by Depeche Mode – 1984

Perception or Reality?

Perceptions can be deceiving. You may have heard the expression "one man's trash is another man's treasure"? Well, sometimes a person's attribute can be mistaken for a flaw. Perception, also referred to as a bias, is an inclination or an outlook often misunderstood. Here is how some people might perceive each of the generations.

Traditionalists

Attributes	***Misunderstood***
Frugal	*Cheap*
Technology-challenged	*Slow*
Conservative	*Closed-minded*
Patriotic	*Right-winged*
Dedicated	*Naive*

Boomers

Attributes	*Misunderstood*
Ambitious	*Dog-eat-dog*
Competitive	*Cutthroat*
Consumerism	*Selfish*
Good communicator	*Dominator*
Loves to work	*Get a life!*
Responsible	*Controlling*
Optimistic	*La-la land*
Assertive	*Aggressive*
Smart	*Know-it-all*

Generation X

Attributes	*Misunderstood*
Highly self-reliant	*Exclusive*
Determined	*Intense*
Dedicated parent	*Overprotective*
Good understanding of money	*Cheap*
Pragmatic	*Hard-nosed*
Self-starter	*Overachiever*
Skeptical	*Cynical and negative*
Work/Life balance	*Slacker*
High standards	*Hard to please*

Millennials

Attributes	***Misunderstood***
Highly educated	*Arrogant*
Highly social	*Goof-off*
Tech-savvy	*Impatient/Intolerant*
Entrepreneurial	*Rules do not apply*
Purpose-driven	*Unrealistic*
Career-focused	*Self-absorbed*
High expectation	*Entitled*
Flexibility	*Lazy*
High self-esteem	*Rude*

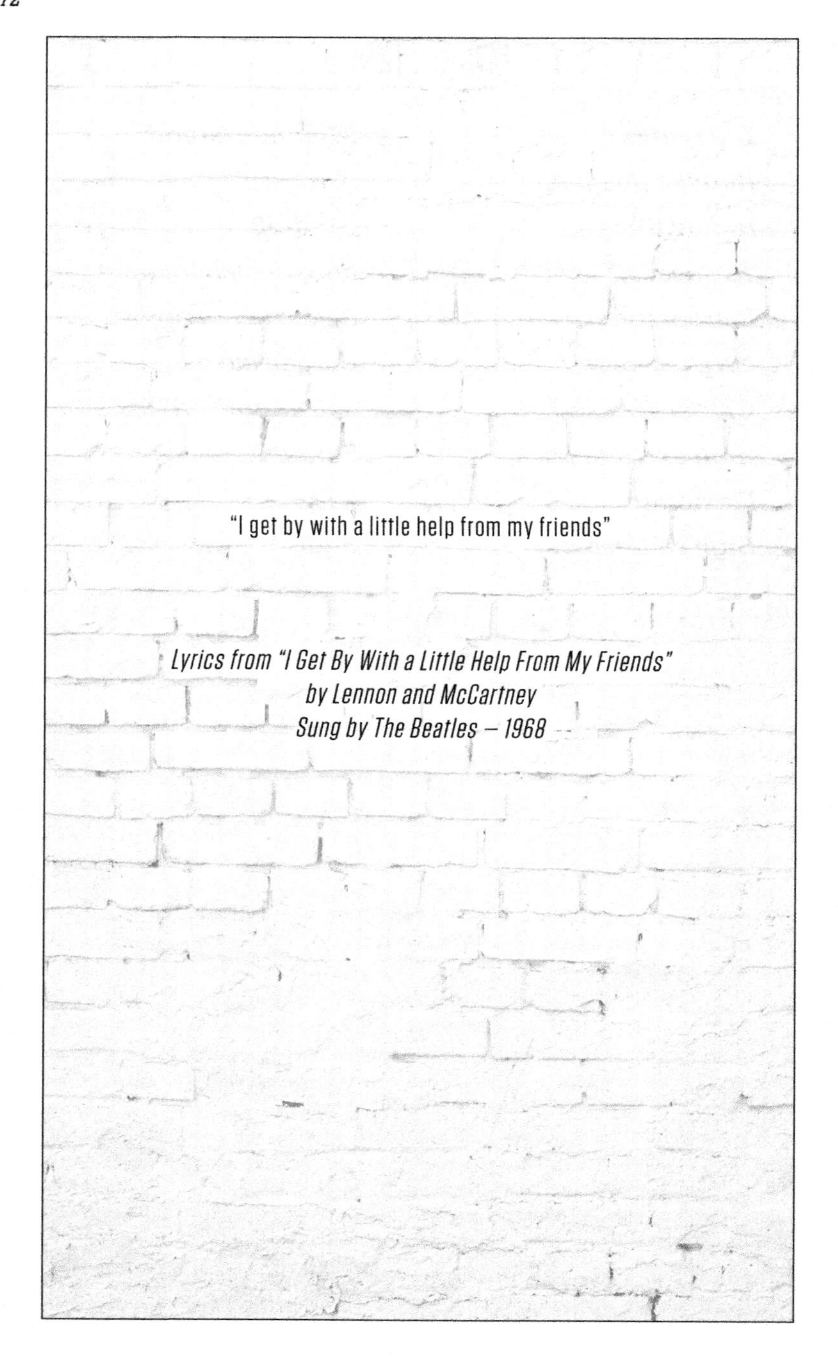
"I get by with a little help from my friends"
Lyrics from "I Get By With a Little Help From My Friends"
by Lennon and McCartney
Sung by The Beatles – 1968

Change

Everything Changes. Or Does It?

> *I asked my friend and fellow speaker, Angie Noel, to contribute the following sections on Change and the Future of Work. Angie calls herself an enlightened HR Executive and Speaker who encourages audiences to lead with mission.*

For the first time in modern history, it is possible that an organization could have employees (and/or volunteers) ranging in age from 18 to 70 serving the organization. While Traditionalists and Gen Z make up a relatively small percentage of the workforce right now, the spread between Boomers and Millennials is enough to keep businesses on their toes trying to figure out how to effectively manage, engage and communicate with the 18-year-old, the 70-year-old and everyone in between. There is much debate, with a fair amount of hype, about the subject of managing the generations at work. So much, in fact, that many companies have been left wondering just how literally they should take the ever-increasing "research," "data," and "expert" opinion being generated on the topic. On one extreme, are the companies that have decided to "Google-ize" everything they can, from nap pods to free food. And on the other, are those with their heads in the proverbial sand.

But what's really changing? As Karen has laid out in previous chapters, every generation enters the workforce with their own attitudes and ideas, beliefs and ethics, perspective and opinion. Each brings along some of the unique influences of their youth, their collective strengths and ideals (aspirations) to the world of work as it exists upon their arrival. And all of them bring the naivety and idealism afforded once in a lifetime to the youth of every generation.

So if every generation enters the workforce hell-bent on making it their own, why does it feel as if the world of work as we've known it is being completely upended? Because it is.

On its own, managing the generations might be more of an interesting social experiment, but organizations aren't just dealing with generations in the workplace. Companies in every industry are also facing radical advancements in technology that have changed the pace of change and are challenging every aspect of business as we know it. Over the last few decades, technological advances alone have accelerated at a pace unlike any other in the history of work (the world). We have seen the introduction of the personal computer, the Internet and the smartphone; each of which has dramatically changed (reshaped) the way we work and live. We've moved from typewriters and telephones to PCs and wearables in a relatively short period of time. We now live and work in a world that few (youngest Boomers) could have even imagined 30 years ago when they entered the workforce.

Today, we have organizations scrambling to catch up, keep up and get a little ahead of the technological curve (if even remotely possible right now) while redesigning how, where and why work is done. Defining the new world of work is no easy task on its own. However, it is, in fact, what organizations are challenged with doing, all while trying to understand the implications of having multiple, distinct generations in the workplace. It's a recipe for a perfect storm, which may call for a perfect drink.

So What's Really Changed

That Was Then

- Traditional hierarchy with a clear promotional ladder
- Command and control leadership – "because I'm the boss and I said so"
- 9am to 5pm office hours – 40+ hours per week
- Work totally done AT YOUR DESK
- Profit above all else

This Is Now

- Career lattice/Multiple careers/Career flexibility/ Freelance
- Collaborative teams
- Work/Life balance
- Location independence
- Meaningful work/Purpose at work

Everyone's Freaking Out...A Little

"The Millennials are coming! The Millennials are coming!" It might just be the best workforce battle cry since the Boomers' "Don't Trust The Man." It may also be the greatest distraction ever needed. As the Millennials enter the workforce with all the skills, attributes and attitudes given to them by their Boomer and Gen Xer parents, they've sort of become the poster children for all of the radical changes and social angst happening right now.

The truth is that everyone is freaking out a little and trying to find their place in this new world of work.

Boomers are Freaking Out

Boomers have had their eye on the retirement prize throughout their entire, loyal, dedicated career only to have their savings decimated in the Great Recession of 2007-2009. This means that some are having to work a little longer than planned to realize the fruits of their career labor. Still other Boomers are hanging out in the workplace, even if only part-time or as volunteers, because their identity has been so attached to their work. It's just who they are. Either way, learning to talk tech, communicate in 140 characters or less, while mastering Facebook may not have been part of the original plan. But Boomers are nothing if not determined and adaptive.

What's Freaking Boomers Out?

- I've worked hard and I'm ready to retire.
- Can I afford to retire?

- Who am I without work?
- Look at me! I am not invisible.
- I have knowledge and experience.
- What is my legacy; do these young kids even care?

Gen Xers are Freaking Out

Gen Xers are probably the most adaptable, having been both influenced by Boomer leaders and played a big part in the information revolution of the World Wide Web. But even Gen Xers are freaking out a little with all of the change happening in the workplace. The Gen Xer came in to the workforce with very low expectations from their Boomer and Traditionalist bosses. Independent, distrustful, free agents that had radical ideas about sharing information freely, the Gen Xer would have to be patient and play by the Boomer's rules if they hoped to advance in their respective companies/industry/field. More than a handful decided to ditch the ladder and "dot-com" their way to success on their own terms. They have paid their dues and as Boomers are beginning to relinquish key leadership roles the Gen Xer is reaping the financial and socio-economic seeds of their patience. But even Gen Xers are freaking out a little with all of the change happening in the workplace.

Gen Xers will work hard, no doubt, but they are being handed the corporate reigns during massive transition and too much time away from the family just isn't worth it to this cohort. As the 'middle child,' Gen Xers find themselves sandwiched between two very large groups of leaders. Those above them retiring at about ten thousand a day and those below them with minimal leadership experience who want what they've worked years for in a matter of months. Gen Xers will be the good 'middle child' though and do what needs to be done. After all, their work life probably mirrors their home life responsibilities of caring for aging parents and younger children. Without much fanfare, the Gen Xer will get it done.

What's Freaking Gen Xers Out?

- Debt
- Savings/Retirement
- Work/Life balance
- Boomers
- Millennials
- Aging parents/Young children

Millennials are Freaking Out...Sort of

Millennials may be the only generation not freaking out just yet. After all, they can be, do and have anything their little hearts desire, right? At least that's what they've been taught. As a generation raised with hyper-involved parents, sporting a "you are the most amazing and special person ever created" self-esteem, they're showing up in the workplace ready to change the world with all that specialness—completely unaware of the skills they lack to do it. So if they aren't freaking out a little it's likely that they just aren't aware yet that they should be! Leadership is not an easy role for any generation and this group is going to be thrust into roles they may or may not be ready for. Organizations have not gotten the leadership development thing right for years—and it would be naive to assume anything will change in the short run. This means that Millennials may have to own their own development and preparation for the many opportunities that lie ahead.

Many Millennials report feeling that organizations seem to be buying into the stereotypes and coddling them with low expectations; the truth is that this tech-savvy, globally connected and innovative cohort may very well be the savior generation *(no pressure!)* Millennials have come of age in an era of seemingly limitless tech expansion, creativity and opportunities. They quite literally do not see limits to the problems that can be solved through technology and collaboration. With little concern for the "old-school rules" and authoritarian hierarchy, Millennials are going to push the envelope in industries in dire need of pushing. As they make their way into the many leadership roles waiting for them, Millennials are going to be challenged head-on with issues impacting government, healthcare and human rights, among others. And we have every reason to believe that they will be ready.

Speaking of pressure...this generation has plenty of it. Being told you can be, do and have anything your heart desires sets a pretty high bar for success. When the expectations are high and everything is an option, there's a ton of pressure to choose wisely and perform well. Growing up in the Facebook era hasn't helped. FB exposed Millennials to the picture-perfect, selfie-taking, overnight uber-successful, save-the-world entrepreneur that never existed standard (role model). The internet allowed anyone to be anything and there has been no shortage of "fakes" with slick content marketing strategies telling and selling Millennials (all of us really) three simple steps to fame, fortune and inner peace. This generation has very high expectations for themselves. They want to change the world and anything less may simply not be worth their time.

What's Freaking Millennials Out?

- Finding work
- School loans/debt
- Purpose, purpose, purpose
- I have to do something amazing/I cannot be ordinary
- Ambition addiction
- Choice overload
- Training

If the world of work is changing and everyone's freaking out a little, then we're probably headed in the right direction. After all, nothing fabulous ever came out of any generation maintaining the status quo, right?

The "Future of Work" is Now

The future of work has become quite the catchphrase lately. It is used in reference to both the tremendous advancements in technology changing the way we physically do work such as the growth of artificial intelligence, as well as, when discussing the expectations of the multiple generations and the modern workforce. The problem I have with the phrase "future of work" is that it gives the impression that we're all headed for a major "change" that will culminate in some great mystical workforce of the future. Cue music…du du duuuu! The reality is that the future of work is now! We're in it. It's not going to change…it is change. Maybe we like the idea of deferring it and pushing it out to some moment in the future because we aren't quite ready for it yet (can't quite wrap our brains around it)? I don't know. But what I do know is that Millennials aren't children that are headed to the workforce; they are adults that are already here influencing the way we do just about everything. Baby Boomers aren't going to retire; they're retiring at a clip of about ten thousand a day right now. Gen Xers aren't going to assume leadership roles; they're in the C-suite, running things right now. And technology isn't something that's coming that we need to prepare for; it's here, now, giving us the ability to do things we couldn't have dreamed of a few years ago.

I think the real challenge then is that it is happening now and it's all happening so fast. Organizations haven't historically been known for their ability to adapt quickly and then there's that pesky element of human behavior we must contend with. All the research and theory in the world won't change the fact that human beings are, well, human. And history has proven our ability to accept and embrace diverse perspectives that challenge our values, our way of thinking or being can be, let's just say, uncomfortable at best. Often there's a fair amount of denial, resistance and conflict that precedes any level of acceptance. And what could be more threatening to our way of being than having our work values, communication styles and habits challenged? Whether it be by the "next" generation, technology/artificial intelligence or change itself, a threat is a threat.

The other challenge, I think, is defining exactly what "it" is that is causing such disruption and anxiety. And this is where I, personally, think the Millennial generation gets a bad rap. It's hard to put a label on the massive amount of change coming from every direction that has become the new normal for most of us. So it's easy to point to the newcomer raised on technology that seems to be challenging our beliefs about work and blame them for our discomfort. Enter the phrase "generational conflict." "Generational conflict" has gained nearly as much press as generations in the workplace in recent years. And it's what you might expect to happen when these distinctly different philosophies about work collide at work. But is generational conflict fact or fiction? It may be a little of both, depending on the culture of any given organization.

Fortunately, for all of our generational differences, we have a lot more in common than some would have us believe. And if we're going to successfully navigate the rapidly changing world of work, we have to figure out what drives and motivates all of us. Luckily, surveys tell us that we all, regardless of generation, tend to want the same core things from our work:

- *Fair compensation*
- *Challenging work*
- *Opportunities for growth*
- *Meaningful work, i.e. work that has a positive impact*
- *Recognition*
- *Respect*
- *Being part of something bigger than ourselves*
- *The ability to contribute*
- *Organizational honesty and transparency*
- *Open communication*

Regardless of generational differences, the one indisputable truth is that whether Boomer, Xer, Millennial or Gen Z, we're all human and we're all in this together, which is fantastic! The real "future of work" is not about generational labels, differences or conflict.

The real future of work is about:

- *Agility*
- *Flexibility*
- *Diversity*

- *Creativity*
- *Curiosity*
- *Appreciation*
- *Purpose*
- *Passion*

And maintaining our humanity as the pace of change and technology continue to encourage us along on one of the greatest journeys of our time.

The generations in the workforce are challenging us to rethink the world of work and technology is forcing us to change it now. And at the end of the day, we'll likely do what we've always done. Some of us will resist and hold tight to "the good old days." Some of us will eagerly adopt the changes and ask for more, while most of us will simply adapt. Because in the end, regardless of generation, we're all human and that's just what we do.

"Don't it always seem to go that
you don't know what you've got till it's gone-
they paved paradise
and they put up a parking lot."

Lyrics from "Big Yellow Taxi"
and song by Joni Mitchell – 1970

Generations in the Workplace

Traditionalists in the Workplace

Setting the Foundation for U.S. Workforce from the Top Down

As the last of the Traditionalists were being born, the country was winding down from WWII. By most accounts, the U.S. entrance into the conflict had won the war, and this "military way of doing things" influenced the way work was done, even off the battlefield.

At the time, organizational structure in a business was military-like and hierarchical, with power flowing vertically and upward, and employees were departmentalized. All employees followed a chain of command. For instance, the CEO had the final say on operations in all divisions, but each department had a manager who ran day-to-day operations and ultimately reported to the CEO. Just like the military, where every soldier answers to his commanding officer and the president of the United States is at the top of the chain as commander-in-chief, this is what the workplace resembled during the Traditionalist era. While most Traditionalists have since retired, their workplace legacy has endured.

Work style Traditionalists brought to the workplace in the 50s and 60s

- *Top-down management style*
- *Hierarchical leadership style*
- *Clear chain of command*
- *"If it ain't broke, don't fix it"*
- *There is a "right" way and a "wrong" way*
- *Conflict avoidance*
- *Conservative approach to work*
- *Work hard to maintain job security*
- *Training happens on the job, not in the classroom*
- *Authority is based on seniority*
- *Work hard, pay your dues*
- *Respect authority*
- *Company first, above all*

If you want a taste for what it was like working in America in the 1950s, I suggest you rent *Mad Men* (Netflix) and dive into the first season.

The early 1950s was a time where conformity ruled, and women and minorities did not share spaces with "the men." TV shows of the era portrayed the loving and dutiful wife, a.k.a. June Cleaver, at home cooking and cleaning, and happily greeting her hard-working husband when he returned in the evening. Shows such as *Donna Reed*, *Father Knows Best*, and *Leave It to Beaver* were the rage. The workplace was a man's world, filled with rules, defined office work hours, face-time meetings, and obligations. Work was the first and primary interest of all those employed—the boss ruled and the worker was committed to work first and family second.

> *The Traditionalist style of management was a major part of the U.S. workforce for many years. Over time, the Boomers tweaked it, Generation X tried to change it—and got angry—and now it's the Millennials who are really shaking things up!*

Keys to working with Traditionalists today on the job and as volunteers

- *Provide consistent rules and clear procedures*
- *Ensure no surprises*
- *Keep them busy*
- *Assign meaningful work*
- *Focus on their skills and ability*
- *Provide networking within your organization so they can feel a part of the culture*
- *Get them out in the community to share their wisdom and stories*
- *Listen to them*
- *Ask them about their lives*

Boomers in the Workplace

Adapting to the new World of Work

Each day 10,000 Baby Boomers are reaching the age of 65, according to Pew Research Center's 2016 estimate. Although the youngest Boomers are 53—and in their work prime—50% of Boomers who are working today will be eligible for retirement in the next three years.

Many Boomers have been with their organizations in various roles for over 30 years and, in some cases, even 40 years. In a Boomer's work lifetime, there have been years of relationship building, years of successes and failures, years of experiences, and years of insights gained that need to be passed along to future teams if an organization is to thrive.

Work style Boomers brought to the workplace in the 80s and 90s

- *Just do it – Get it done*
- *Bottom line it*
- *Team-building*
- *Conflict avoidance*
- *Long hours at work*
- *Micro-managers*
- *Process-driven*
- *Yearly reviews*
- *Uncomfortable with feedback*
- *Struggles with non-traditional work styles of younger generation*

When you think about a person's career over the course of decades, you realize they have ideas and knowledge not written down in reports or summaries. This valuable "experience knowledge" is the stuff we carry around in our heads that we just know.

This deeper knowledge is called perspective and contains invaluable insight that should be passed on to the newer members of the work team.

Here are a few questions to discuss when thinking about the Boomers leaving for retirement and the knowledge gaps that will leave in your organization.

- *What is the Boomer's perspective on the future of the organization?*
- *What "Boomer" knowledge do we want to retain?*
- *How do we break it down to pass it down?*
- *What are the critical skills that your team performs that the Boomer can help enhance?*
- *How many people are competent and how many need some help?*

When working on transferring knowledge, it is important to have open lines of communication between younger and seasoned employees. Mutual respect and trust must be established so the more inexperienced employee does not feel intimidated and afraid to admit that they do not know something. Conversely, the Boomer must be willing to open up and share.

This sharing of information and perspective needs to be a two-way street. Although it is important for Boomers to open up about their experiences in the workplace, Millennials and Gen Xers have much to teach the older generations about communicating and marketing.
An exciting phenomenon is taking place today in our multigenerational workplace. Reverse mentoring is

taking root as the Baby Boomers seek out Millennials and Gen Xers to help them understand and use the latest in technology, social media, and even to listen to their perspective on the marketplace and disruptions.

For reverse mentoring to work, organizations must receive a "buy-in" from the top leaders. Taking the time and pairing the right teams together is critical. Each member of the team must be committed to making the process work and must be open to sharing ideas and knowledge. That said, there needs to be some ground rules established, spelling out expectations. Each member of the team has to practice their listening skills—yes, Boomers, you have to stop talking and listen so you can learn from someone younger than yourself.

Reverse mentoring is collaboration on steroids! With it, organizations can create an atmosphere of trust that is both critical and exciting.

"It's my turn
To see what I can see
I hope you'll understand
This time's just for me
Because it's my turn
With no apologies"

Lyrics from "My Turn"
by Carole Bayer Sager
Sung by Diana Ross – 1980

Gen Xers in the Workplace

Time to Step in and Lead

Generation X entered the workforce when the Boomers were in their prime, and early on, there were not many areas for this generation to flourish—except, of course, in technology!

Because many Gen Xers learned independence early in life, this attribute turned out to be a valuable trait, so Gen Xers progressed in their work and in the world. As writer Mary Donohue emphatically writes in her recent blog post in the *Huffington Post* "Forget Millennials and Boomers. Gen X will Save the Workplace":

> *Gen X is your bread and butter. They have worked through more recessions than their parents or grandparents ever did. Most often they are executive leaders who are on the cusp of becoming the C-class, but aren't thriving in the workplace. The closer these workers get to 55 the more their knowledge becomes invaluable to your organization and to your customers. They are your intellectual capital.*

Work style Gen Xers brought—and continue to bring—to the workplace

- *Choices*
- *Collaboration*
- *Rethinking things*
- *Options*

- *Flexibility*
- *Innovation*
- *Fun*

Because many Gen Xers had early contact with the "real world," they are highly self-reliant and positioned to take on leadership in all organizations—corporate, non-profit, and community. As a whole, they are serious about meeting commitments, have a strong sense of purpose, and are highly resilient. Gen X is the generation who wants options/choices since they don't want to be cornered into just one and only one single way of doing something. They are innovative, creative, and insightful. These qualities position them for great leadership in an era of disruptive thinking. Gen X values new ideas and "out of the box" thinking.

As leaders today, they must help organizations become more collaborative. They must continue to ask great questions and get others excited and engaged in work and projects. They must embrace complexity and continue to seek new answers and new disruptions. And they must keep up their need for authenticity, purpose, and mission in the workplace and world.

Keys to working with Gen X today

- *Give them freedom and independence*
- *Allow time to pursue other interests*
- *Keep up with technology*
- *Keep it informal*
- *Direct communication works best*
- *Laugh and have fun*

Millennials in the Workplace

New Kids Shaking up the Block

I have been speaking on "Generations in the Workplace" for nearly 10 years now. And I can remember back in 2008 when there were just a handful of Millennials in the audience. Today, my audiences are filled with more people 35 and under as the number of Millennials in the workplace continues to increase.

At the present time, nearly half of the U.S. workforce is composed of Millennials, a generation that is shaking things up and changing the world of work. It is important we understand this dynamic group if we expect to get along in the work world. We are discovering that Millennials are seeking a multi-dimensional lifestyle that satisfies both their work and personal lives. They are definitely impatient and want to proceed along their career paths more rapidly than Boomers or even Gen Xers.

Work style Millennials are bringing to the workplace

- *Casual and informal*
- *Team-oriented work*
- *Rewards extra effort*
- *Inclusiveness*
- *Culture of authenticity*
- *More fun and collaboration*

Today, you have to meet Millennials where they are if you want to succeed. Yes, it does take more energy, but if you invest the extra time, you're more likely to keep them in your organization and grow their talent. We must take a look at the workplace through their perspective in order to understand what they are about. The bottom line is that forcing them to conform to your way will only push them away.

Keys to working with Millennials today: Understand what motivates them!

To understand what motivates Millennials and how to work with and manage them, you need to consider what they want in the workplace. The things listed here should not surprise you...don't we all want them? Here is a sample of what will likely get Millennials excited about work:

- ***Embracing Diversity and Inclusion*** – *Millennials want to work with positive peers, be treated with respect, and be asked for their input. People have raised the question, "What's the difference between diversity and inclusion?" It can be summed up this way: Diversity is like getting an invitation to the dance. Inclusion is being asked to dance once you get there.*

- ***Challenge*** – *Millennials want to work on demanding projects with an engaged team that cares about the outcome of their task, embraces complexity, and seeks disruptions.*

- ***Learning*** – *Millennials want to gain knowledge from a variety of tasks, so they can grow their careers quickly.*

- ***Career goals*** – *Millennials want to be able to clearly see their future and their career path in the organization where they work.*

- ***Feedback*** *– Millennials want feedback on how they are doing, and they want to hear it often.*
- ***Transparency*** *– Millennials want to know how their performance will be measured. They like structure and systems, and they want to understand by what metrics they will be judged.*
- ***Techno 24/7*** *– Millennials want the ability to leverage technology when working…anytime, anyplace.*
- ***Tap into Social Platforms*** *– Millennials are social beings; they want to use social platforms to grow the organization's employee brand.*
- ***Results-Oriented Flexibility*** *– Millennials want to be evaluated on their finished work, not on how, when, or where the work is done.*
- ***Access*** *– Millennials want open and constant communication with their boss (and their boss's boss, and so on).*
- ***Friendly Environment*** *– Millennials want to have friends at work, and they want the workplace to be a pleasant and social place. They prefer to work on teams rather than as individuals. Millennials want to interact directly and often with their managers (feedback works) and coworkers. They want to work in a friendly place where they feel a sense of acceptance and enjoyment in the workplace environment.*
- ***Core Values*** *– Millennials want to identify with the company's core values and work with people who share their priorities. They are very willing to leave a company if its purpose does not align with their own values. Anything less would mean they are not individually authentic, and, therefore, cannot relate to managers and fellow team members in an authentic way.*

- ***Sharing and Caring** – Millennials want interaction and collaboration at work. Sharing information and comments are a big part of their day-to-day activities.*

As Dennis Nally, head of human resources at PricewaterhouseCoopers, puts it:

> *"This Millennial generation is not just looking for a job. They're not just looking for salary and financial benefits. They're looking for skill development. They're looking for mobility. They're looking for opportunities to acquire different skills and to move quickly from one part of an organization to another. How you manage that sort of talent and how you deal with their expectations is very different from what's been done in the past."*

Boomer and Gen X company leaders may find it frustrating to manage Millennials. The biggest challenge for any organization is to be open and willing to make a shift towards new priorities in the workspace. The workplace must bend to accommodate the Millennial mindset. Today, the need for young talent is critical for an organization's success. It is a competitive market and the ability to recruit and retain the best and the brightest is necessary.

Millennials have the ability to transform the disruption of the workplace into profit for a company. First, however, managers and marketers must be willing to adapt and change to fit their needs, and this is where I have encountered the biggest resistance.

Who's up for the challenge?

"I'm a survivor
I'm not gon' give up
I'm not gon' stop
I'm gon' work harder
I'm a survivor
I'm gonna make it
I will survive
Keep on survivin'"

Lyrics from "Survivor"
by Beyoncé
Sung by Destiny's Child – 2001

All Together Now

For All Generations: Unwritten Rules at Work

Reality bites…and the reality is that today there are still powerful "Unwritten Rules" in every organization that stand in the way of success. These are the Unwritten Rules for career advancement. All generations—not just the Millennials—need to be aware of advancement strategies and recognize opportunities to make key decisions about their career options.

Here are my suggestions for conquering the Unwritten Rules:

1. **Be Observant:** Begin a new job or new department or team by closing your mouth and opening your

eyes and ears. Observe how things get done. Your workplace success requires a deep understanding of how the organization or new team functions and how decisions are made. Be fully aware of the politics and notice where the political landmines exist. Political know-how is important...and those who fail to develop such skills are often the ones who get left behind.

2. **Discover:** Now that you understand your organization, find out where you fit into the big picture. Every organization has a culture that sets the tone for the types of people who are hired. You need to know why you were hired, where you fit into the organization, and how your superior sees your career path in the organization.

3. **Master THEIR Way before Suggesting YOUR Way:** Be patient. Don't jump in and start making suggestions on how to do things better. Master the system, take your time, and understand the process before you give your suggestions to change the system. Don't start off with criticisms.

4. **Share your Goals:** Speak up and effectively communicate your career goals, your ideas, desired assignments, and when the time is right, ask to be considered for promotion.

5. **Build your Relationships and Grow your Circle of Influencers:** Start your list of 25 people you admire, people you can learn from—leaders, gatekeepers, and people in your organization who have enthusiasm and ideas. Then join organizations, formal and informal networking groups, and, as Keith Ferazzi once said, "Never eat alone." Make it a point of having lunch with members of your team and those in your circle of influence.

6. **Be a Giver:** Figure out how to cultivate your list of 25 and grow the relationship BEFORE you ask for advice or a favor. Share your talents (perhaps in technology) and be open to teaching others.

7. **Increase your visibility:** Volunteer to give a presentation! Did that scare you? Do your homework—practice, practice, practice—and make it a great one. Become known and get involved.

8. **Take pride in how you show up.** Although we are seeing a more flexible work trend—dress still matters! How you dress for work is even more complicated today than in years past. The casual dress trend combined with today's increased focus on "snug-fitting" clothes makes it clear that deciding how to dress for work takes some thought and preparation.

Every business has a culture and every culture has a costume. Make sure your day-to-day outfits fit your company's look and feel...and are "company appropriate."

Some professional cultures still require suits while others, such as the tech cultures, are more relaxed... and if you are Mark Zuckerberg, you may even get by with a grey hoodie! Be mindful of the image you want to project at work with clients and peers, and choose outfits based on cues from those you admire.

"Remember, whatever you do at work, no matter how small it is, has your signature on it! Make it clear, bold, and easy to read!"

Karen McCullough

"Celebration – Let's all celebrate and have a good time
Celebration – We gon' celebrate and have a good time

It's time to come together
It's up to you, what's your pleasure?
Everyone around the world come on"

Lyrics from "Celebrate"
by Kool and the Gang – 1980

A Final Word From Karen

Grow Your Circles: Stop, Listen, Connect

Over the past decade, our country and the world have clearly been marked by changes of all kinds—in security, the economy, technology, weather patterns, politics, social policy, environment and yes, the generations. Some of the changes have been exciting, (AirBnB, Uber, Square) while others have been scary, shocking, and in some cases quite devastating.

Yes, we are living through dynamic times that are both inspiring and troubling, often in the same moment.

In the face of such dramatic change we know how easy it is to get discouraged, disappointed, and overwhelmed. But in the face of such unprecedented change, in addition to big hurdles, there are also big opportunities and advantages—generational advantages that connect us to each other.

I have worked across the country, for all types of organizations and I have met many great people...from all the generations. Many of the younger individuals opened my mind and my curiosity and they have enriched my life and shown me another way! Many of the wise and highly experienced elders have reminded me that what goes up also can go down and then up again. Life takes us through many cycles and we need wisdom and patience to endure.

I now urge you to grow your circle of influence and include all the generations in your world. Learn how to ask good questions and then practice listening to the knowledge and stories. It's through the stories that life takes on meaning.

As we read with Millennials and 70-year-old intern, Paul, once we get to know people on a level deeper than the surface, we begin to connect because of our similarities, not our differences, and both sides learn and grow!

Before we judge, stop and listen. Look for the common threads that connect us all to a greater purpose. Before we judge, honor those that came before us, paving the way for us to grow. Before we judge, listen and learn from those younger than us, as they open our eyes and our minds to what's ahead.

Generations Rock is about all the generations sharing their quirks and attributes. *Generations Rock* is about us—you and me—and the stories that connect us to each other. I urge you to seek out those different from you, ask questions, listen and continue to learn grow and evolve. And remember, have a great time out there changing the world!

Resources

Addicted To Ambition: 3 Ways Millennials Can Manage Their Stress by Caroline Beaton
Bossy Pants by Tina Fey
CNN – American Generations Fast Facts Deloitte Millennial Survey 2017
Global Human Capital 2016 – Deloitte University Press
Executive Presence by Sylvia Ann Hewlett
Harvard Business Publications
Huffington Press
Fast Company
Fearless after Fifty by Rumbaugh/Marchildon
Forbes Magazine
Millennials @ Work by Chip Espinoza
Pew Research Center
Ryan Jenkins' Podcasts
Sunday Morning with Jane Pauley
The Incentive Research Foundation
Time Magazine
Unwritten by Laura Hillenbrand

Contributor

Angie Noel is a speaker and leadership coach on a mission to end human misery...at work. An "enlightened" HR leader of 20 years, Angie is convinced that most people want to be engaged in work they feel connected to and enjoy doing. Through her programs on leadership and engagement, she inspires people and organizations to shift perspective, get engaged and lead with what matters most to love the work you do and live a life you love.

Check her out at LeadingWithMission.com

Author

Author Karen McCullough is called a Branding Expert, a Social Media Enthusiast, and a Millennial Evangelist, and she's on a mission to get you excited about change. She's an award-winning speaker who inspires and empowers organizations and individuals to evolve, grow, and realize their true potential for excellence.

For the last 18 years, Karen has been developing creative solutions and implementing innovative methods for motivating people to embrace and thrive with CHANGE.

> *"What a joy it was to have Karen McCullough speak at our conference! Not only is she a bundle of energy, she is a fiery Millennial Evangelist who inspires, challenges and inspires change! Attendees poured out of her sessions energized, with concrete take-aways. Not only does Karen bring branding, social media and futuristic ideas to each session…she lives it and it is evident the moment she steps foot onto the property!"*
>
> Juliann Talley, Director of Events and Education – 6/15/17

Connect with Karen and Discover for Yourself.

She is a Proven Winner.

KarenMcCullough.com • Karen@KarenMcCullough.com

Made in the USA
Middletown, DE
26 April 2022

64750485R00070